# My Life is My Responsibility

Insights for Conscious Living

Peter Mulraney

Copyright © 2017 Peter Mulraney

All rights reserved.

This book may not be reproduced in whole or in part, except by a reviewer who may quote brief passages in a review, without the written permission of the publisher.

ISBN 13: 978-0-6482523-2-0

This edition published 2018

*To the generous members of the Unsplash community,
whose images grace these pages.*

# Contents

| | |
|---|---:|
| Introduction | 1 |
| My life is my responsibility | 3 |
| Attend to your own business | 5 |
| Living your life without a clear intention | 7 |
| Sometimes, you need to be in the dark | 9 |
| Nothing stays forever | 11 |
| Heaven or hell? Your choice | 13 |
| Being alone | 15 |
| Have you ever wondered? | 17 |
| Expand your presence | 19 |
| Forgotten does not mean broken | 21 |
| All events are neutral | 23 |
| Just because you believe it | 25 |
| Darkness allows us to see the beauty of our lights | 27 |
| Those who work with love have no need for guns | 29 |
| It's not the truth | 31 |
| Are you sure it's worth getting upset about? | 33 |
| Sinking beneath the surface waves of life | 35 |
| There are times when you have to wait | 37 |
| Death is an event for observers | 39 |
| Look for the beauty – it's always there | 41 |
| I am beautiful | 43 |
| Nature is waiting for you | 45 |
| When you're angry, it's not about me | 47 |
| Appreciate the people in your life – just as they are | 49 |
| To be in the present moment | 51 |
| I am not here to judge or be judged | 53 |

| | |
|---|---|
| Happiness is an inside job | 55 |
| Appreciate what you have | 57 |
| The secret to forgiveness | 59 |
| Shit happens | 61 |
| No-one takes anything from you when they leave | 63 |
| It doesn't matter what anybody else thinks about you | 65 |
| It's only when you're aware | 67 |
| All endings lead to new beginnings | 69 |
| Words have a power that can be used | 71 |
| The power of the pause | 73 |
| It's okay to start with loving yourself | 75 |
| There's nothing wrong with having an opinion | 77 |
| There are no special roles for spiritual pilgrims | 79 |
| When you're caught in the drama | 81 |
| There are no ordinary moments | 83 |
| What is it that you think you can control? | 85 |
| It's time to take a look behind the curtain | 87 |
| It doesn't actually matter what you choose | 89 |
| You get to choose the level at which you experience life | 91 |
| One act of love inspires another | 93 |
| One person living authentically allows others | 95 |
| Sometimes you get to plant seeds | 97 |
| We have access to a level of knowing | 99 |
| There is a much bigger plan at play | 101 |
| Life is a field of possibilities | 103 |
| The spiritual journey happens in the here and now | 105 |
| Further reading | 107 |
| A note from Peter | 109 |

| | |
|---|---:|
| Photographic credits | 110 |
| Other Titles by Peter Mulraney | 112 |

# Introduction

Conscious living involves being aware of what's going on in your life and, more importantly, what's going on in your mind.

How you experience life depends on what you choose to believe.

If you never take the time to examine your beliefs, or to question your assumptions, you end up living unconsciously. When you liv unconsciously, you live your life according to somebody else's beliefs. You end up trying to meet somebody else's expectations and not your own.

We all inherit beliefs from our family, from the culture we live in, from the schooling we receive, and from the messages we are exposed to in the media.

There is nothing wrong with that. It's all part of the plan. You have to start somewhere when you arrive on the planet. But, at some point, you'll be called to move beyond that starting point. A lot of us resist that call. It sounds unsettling, like too much trouble.

Life often gives us quite a shove in our mid-thirties: a mid-life crisis. Some of us pay attention.

What I noticed was a whisper inside that wouldn't go away. It kept inviting me to look within and stop worrying so much about what was going on in the world around me. Sometimes, it would nudge me to read a book by a particular author, or to listen to someone speak, or to undertake a course of study.

When we get these prompts and do something about them, we begin by exploring voices from within our belief bubble. Having been born into a Catholic family, my early exploration involved studying the works of various Catholic authors, but then something happened and I started reading more widely.

I came across *A Course in Miracles* and, several years later, *The Way of Mastery*, both of which encouraged me to examine what I thought was real, and challenged all my beliefs about God and what it meant to be human. Those works started me on the path to accepting responsibility for my life and opened my mind to the possibility that

*My Life is My Responsibility.*

nothing was as I thought or believed it was.

The insights in this book flow from a sense of being aware that you can change the world, but not in the way most of us think about doing that.

Real change happens when you finally accept that there is only one thing that can be changed: how you choose to see things.

My hope, in sharing these insights, is that they may inspire you to question what you have been told, and to spend a few moments contemplating the possibility that things may not be as you have been led to believe.

This book is an invitation to accept responsibility for your life, and to let others accept responsibility for theirs.

A few words on how the book is structured. It's not designed to be read from cover to cover in one sitting, and there is no order in which the insights should be contemplated.

Each chapter has:

- an image which holds the text of the insight,
- a discussion or expansion of that insight,
- a ponder point for you to think about, and
- actions for you to consider in relation to the insight.

I recommend that you keep a journal to record your observations and insights as you work your way through the book.

## My life is my responsibility

Until you come to the point of accepting responsibility for everything that happens in your life, you are not free.

When you refuse to accept that your life is your responsibility, you continue to blame someone or something else for everything that happens to you. You see yourself as a victim of fate, a tyrannical god, controlling people, and natural disasters. You blame your parents, the government, and any person who abused you in any way for how your life has turned out.

Accepting responsibility for your life is both confronting and liberating at the same time.

It's confronting when you have experienced things or committed acts you would rather forget than take responsibility for.

It's liberating because it lets you see that you are never a victim.

How do we go about accepting responsibility for our lives?

One way is to stop thinking of yourself as a human being with a limited lifespan and to see yourself as a spiritual being that chose to incarnate into the human form - for specific learning experiences.

When you look at your life from this perspective, you need to acknowledge that you chose your parents and the circumstances into which you were born.

From this perspective, you also come to appreciate that events happen for you and not to you. Things only happen to you if you see yourself as a victim.

Another way of looking at that is to regard all events as neutral – that is; they happen but they have no intrinsic meaning. The only meaning any event has is the meaning you give it. You are the one who decides whether an event is beneficial, disastrous, or of no consequence.

Accepting responsibility for your life means acknowledging that you have total control over the way in which you respond to any event.

That's why you hear all sorts of gurus telling you that change begins within. They're telling you that although you may not be able to change the world, you can change the way you behave.

Accepting responsibility for your life also means you get to choose what you believe; instead of simply accepting what others tell you to believe.

### Ponder point

So, who or what has control of your life?

You might think you are in control but, unless you're willing to examine your beliefs and habits, you're probably fooling yourself.

### Actions to consider

Spend some time listening to what you say, and what you think but don't say.

Take a look at how you react when people push your buttons.

Start keeping a journal to record your observations.

## Attend to your own business

One of the great temptations of life is to run other people's lives for them. It's a great distraction from running your own.

Have you noticed how parents like to tell their children how to live their lives, even when they're adults with children of their own?

Most of the time you don't even realize you're doing it. Other times you do it on purpose – with the best of intentions, of course. After all, you do know what's best, don't you?

The truth is you don't know what's best for another. It often takes a lifetime of inner work to discover what is best for yourself.

The flip side is you often let other people run your life - whether it's a spouse, a parent, a priest, some politician or the gossip down the street – or, more likely these days, on social media or talkback radio.

Part of taking responsibility for your life is allowing others to take responsibility for their business while you attend to yours.

That doesn't mean that as parents of young children you let them do as they please, but it does mean that as your children grow and mature you need to transfer the responsibility for how they live their lives gradually over to them.

Not always easy but essential. At some point, though, you need to be like the birds and push them out of the nest.

How someone chooses to behave is not your business. What you choose to do about it - that's your business. That's the part you are responsible for.

When we aren't running other people's lives, we often devote our energy to solving the problems of the world or complaining about things we have no influence over – activities which provide distraction or avoidance from the realities of our lives.

Attending to your business, instead of trying to run the world, is actually a lot less stressful than worrying about things you have no control over.

Funny thing is though, when you stop trying to run other people's lives, they seem to do a good job of living them on their own, and you start enjoying your own life more.

♥

## Ponder point

Whose lives are you interfering in? Who are you telling how to live their life or bring up their children?

If you're doing it professionally, keep in mind that doing it as an educator and not as a dictator will always be more effective.

## Actions to consider

Observe how you relate to the people in your life, at home and at work. Are you trying to take care of their business?

Notice whether you let others tell you what to do or what to think. Are you taking care of your business?

Record your observations and thoughts in your journal.

## Living your life without a clear intention.

You can either let the circumstances of your life story dictate the path of your life - or you can choose a specific path for yourself.

If you let your circumstances dictate, they could take you anywhere, because you are relinquishing any control you might have.

This often seems the easier choice, which is why you hear motivational speakers challenge you to get out of your comfort zone. It's called a comfort zone because you don't have to do anything different if you stay there. But, you have to deal with whatever happens, and I hear a lot of people complaining about the hand life has dealt them.

On the other hand, if you set your intention on living a certain kind of life, you signal your desire to the universe, and you can take action to move in that direction.

This takes courage. Often it involves doing something different to everybody around you. It often means people will think (and tell you) that you're crazy or too big for your britches.

One of the interesting things about life is that it comes with an in-built feedback mechanism, which lets you know whether you're on course or need to make a course correction. This means that, when unexpected things happen in your life, you can decide what they mean in terms of your life purpose. If you have a clear intention, you check your progress against your goals, those signposts you set to help

*My Life is My Responsibility.*

you navigate from where you are to where you want to be.

Can you imagine a ship leaving port without a destination marked on the map and a compass? Didn't think so. It makes just as much sense for you to choose a destination before you set sail as well.

When you take responsibility for your life, you're communicating to the universe, and to everyone around you, that you have a clear intention. You're announcing that you're taking ownership of the powers available to you.

❤

**Ponder point**

Are you living your life with a clear intention or blaming your circumstances for the way your life is?

Be honest with yourself but also be gentle. There is no point in beating yourself up.

**Actions to consider**

Take stock of what's going on in your life right now.

Decide if you want things to be different.

Set or reset your intention and decide on the signposts that will help you chart your progress.

Record your observations and thoughts in your journal.

## Sometimes, you need to be in the dark

I suspect we have always been afraid of the dark, in its many forms, and at times that was probably for good reasons, but today it seems we are not all that willing to embrace the dark in any form.

We illuminate our homes with artificial light, as soon as the sun sets, so we will not be in the dark, in effect extending the day well into the night. On one hand that's a good thing. I'm not suggesting you turn your back on progress and switch off the lights. On the other hand, it makes it so easy to fill your life with busyness.

Darkness gives you an opportunity to stop and do that inner work that does not require an external light.

Often, we can't tear ourselves away from our devices, in case we miss out on a snippet of information and find ourselves in the dark about some vital or trivial issue. One wonders how we ever survived in those pre-internet days of information darkness, waiting for the nightly news update or the morning paper to feed our need to know about what was going on in the world.

How did people ever survive when you had to wait days, weeks or even months for news from your friends and relatives in the next town, let alone news from distant places on the other side of the globe?

Sadly, most of it is only noise, distracting you from living your life in the present moment with the people right there with you.

Sometimes darkness comes in the form of anguish, presenting you with questions you'd rather not deal with, so you suppress it with medication or some other addiction, instead of sitting with it and discovering the lesson it's brought to you.

Darkness allows you to step out of the glare of the light and see the things waiting for you in the shadows.

Silence, the form darkness takes in the world of sound, allows you to hear the voice of intuition, which is drowned out by the sea of noise surrounding you every day.

### Ponder point

When was the last time you sat in the dark, unplugged from all your devices, and stayed with an issue until you knew what to do next?

Have you even considered that approach?

### Actions to consider

Set aside a time to sit quietly, with your eyes closed, and listen to what's going on inside you.

Make sitting quietly a regular, daily practice.

Spend a day unplugged from your devices.

Record your observations and thoughts in your journal.

## Nothing stays forever

Life is a flow of ever changing events, moment to moment; yet how often do you stand in its path trying to stop its movement?

People appear in your life for a period; then they leave. Why do you get upset?

Your ideas are popular one day and forgotten or ridiculed the next. Why are you offended?

Something unpleasant arrives for a visit, only to be transformed into a moment of unexpected joy. Why are you surprised?

How often have you found yourself expending energy holding onto people, beliefs and things? Or found yourself expending your energy resisting change?

Pay attention to the parade of the seasons. There is a message there. That's nature's way of reminding you that nothing stays forever.

Even those majestic trees that live for hundreds of years eventually fall to the forest floor and decay back into the soil that grew them.

Every mountain, edifice and monument on the planet is slowly turning to dust.

What makes you think today's troubles will be here tomorrow?

It doesn't matter what's going on in your life; it will pass. Take a moment and recall an earlier time in your life – it's not the same as today, is it?

Your part in the play of life is to notice and experience, and then let go. It's not to hoard and hold on to everything and everyone that comes along.

You won't be staying here forever either, so make the most of your visit and experience as much as you can, instead of lamenting over people and things that have served their purpose in your life and moved on.

❤

### Ponder point

Why do you think resisting change is such a common human behavior?

### Actions to consider

Spend some time identifying issues you are holding on to.

Spend some time identifying people you are holding on to.

Allow yourself to feel the pain of your loss, and then let it go.

Record your observations and thoughts in your journal.

# Heaven or hell? Your choice

Any given circumstance can be perceived as heaven or hell. It all depends on your perspective at the time.

Interestingly, what I perceive as heaven or a blessing you may choose to see as hell or some form of divine punishment. The designation depends on your state of mind and not the actual situation, and on the understanding that heaven and hell are states of mind, and not places you'll find on a map of the cosmos.

If you're in victim mode, where everything happens to you, it's easy to see any situation that does not meet your expectations as being an experience of hell or divine retribution.

When you move beyond victim mode to accepting that you are responsible for your life, nothing ever happens to you. It all happens for you, and when things don't meet your expectations, you stop and wonder what Life is drawing your attention to now, instead of lamenting: why me?

Life happens, and we experience a flow of events. There is no denying that some of the circumstances we encounter are difficult and unpleasant to deal with, but that does not mean we are being punished by a malevolent God, despite what you may have heard preached from a pulpit some place.

No matter what event presents itself, you always have the power to choose how you will respond to it, even if you have forgotten you do.

No circumstance stays forever and, even though you may initially believe you have stumbled into hell, you can always change your mind about a particular circumstance as you become more aware of what it means for you. Or as you become more aware of the details and stop listening to the voice in your head that misinterpreted the whole thing from the start.

One of the interesting findings coming out of brain research is that our minds do not present us with a picture of reality but with an interpretation of reality based upon our stored experiences and beliefs.

There's a warning there. If you apply a negative filter, you'll get a negative result. In other words, if you go about looking for hell, you'll find it everywhere.

I'd rather go about looking for heaven but, as always, the choice is yours.

### Ponder point

How are you choosing to interpret events in your life? Do you look at the facts or go with the voice in your head?

### Actions to consider

Spend some time examining the hell events in your life and ask yourself whether your interpretation of those events is based on opinion or fact.

Consider reframing the way you think about those events and see if there could be another way of seeing them.

Record your observations and thoughts in your journal.

*Being alone is not the same as being lonely.*

## Being alone

We have a word for spending time with yourself – solitude. It's a necessary experience for anyone undertaking the inner journey, and one that all pilgrims choose.

You can find solitude by retreating into your room or going for long walks in nature on your own. When you really want to get away from everybody, you can go on a pilgrimage walk, like the Camino de Santiago, or participate in a silent retreat.

One side of solitude is spending time getting to know and befriend yourself. It's easy to forget that, no matter who else is around, you are always with yourself, and it only makes sense to be your own best friend. Another aspect of solitude is doing things that you enjoy on your own. Things like reading or listening to music or weeding the garden.

If you're not comfortable being alone, maybe it's time to find out why. What are you afraid of finding out if you're silent long enough to hear your own thoughts?

Often, friends mistake your desire for solitude as loneliness and want to take pity on you so you will not be alone. Many do not understand the point of solitude – being with yourself.

Feeling lonely is a natural feeling; nothing to be ashamed of. We are social beings. We enjoy being with other people and miss our friends and lovers when not with them.

My Life is My Responsibility.

If you're feeling lonely, solitude may not help. The cure for loneliness is being with other people. Maybe it's a reminder that you need to get out more and stop spending so much time with yourself.

Once, the life of a mystic was akin to being a hermit. That's no longer the case. Even those of us on the inner journey need the company of friends and fellow pilgrims.

And, let's be honest. We are here to engage with life; not sit in solitude.

Solitude has its purpose but so does having fun and enjoying the company of others.

♥

### Ponder point

Are you using solitude as part of your inner journey or are you afraid of what you might discover if you spend time alone with yourself?

### Actions to consider

Treat yourself to a day of solitude.

Go for a walk in nature.

Record your observations and thoughts in your journal.

## Have you ever wondered?

If we're spirits enjoying an incarnation here on earth, where were we before we were born this time?

This is not something I gave much thought to until I started studying *The Way of Mastery*, in which Jeshua tells us we're always in the Heart of God. In other words, we've never left home. We simply place our attention on our experience of being here.

This made me think of the online virtual world, Second Life, where you sit at your computer but participate in the virtual world via an avatar; that is; you stay at home but place your attention upon your manifestation in the online world.

Jeshua refers to the body as being the communication device required for engaging with the experience of being human. In other words, an avatar.

According to Jeshua, the trap within this game is identifying with your avatar - and we all fall for it until the moment we awaken from the dream and remember who we are.

You can get another perspective on this by reading *Life between Lives* by Dr. Michael Newton, which provides an overview of what Dr. Newton's hypnotherapy patients told him during their sessions.

Interestingly, what Dr. Newton's patients remembered during their past life regression therapy sessions aligns with Jeshua's account.

The theme of their responses was: we are souls that belong to a family of souls that goes on educational field trips together to places like Earth. Each time you come, you take on a different role but a part of your soul never leaves home base. When your part in the field trip is over, the portion of your soul that was invested in the lesson rejoins the part at home base. That's the bit we call dying, when the soul separates from the body or avatar.

When you're back at home base, you review your progress with your guide, much like you review an assignment with a teacher, and then decide on your next assignment before being born again.

Think about that for a moment. It means you never die. It means you pick the circumstances into which you are born for a specific reason, and you bring the value of your previous learning with you.

The trick is, you need to awaken from the dream of being human (or undergo past life regression therapy) to access that soul learning.

❤

### Ponder point

If you are a soul on a field trip, what do you think this particular field trip might be about?

### Actions to consider

Review your life story. Is there a pattern in the events of your life? Is there something that appears to occur over and over again?

Think about the people in your life and the ones that have come and gone. Is there anyone who has or has had a particular influence on you?

Record your observations and thoughts in your journal.

## Expand your presence

You have life experience. You know how to do things. You have knowledge and skills. Your experience is valuable.

You can choose to employ the benefit of your experience to further your own agenda or you can share what you know with others.

Whether you are aware of it or not, you are a centre of influence. You can make a difference if you're willing to expand your presence by being visible; by being generous with what you know.

Generosity or sharing recognises abundance. There is always more than enough to go around.

When you give away what you know by teaching others, paradoxically, you don't lose anything. You still have your knowledge. You still have your skills. You have expanded your presence.

There are many ways of sharing. Sometimes, all it requires is a willingness to offer a helping hand or advice to a friend or family member. At other times, it might be more appropriate to offer your knowledge and skills in the marketplace.

There is nothing wrong with being rewarded for sharing or teaching. Often, recipients place more value on the information they pay for than on advice freely given – even if it's exactly the same information.

This insight is the one that inspires me to write the blog posts and books that allow me to share my knowledge and skills, and to expand my presence.

It's hard to imagine that only a few short years ago most of us were confined within tiny circles of influence. Very few had access to an audience beyond their circle of friends before the digital revolution. Today, any of us can have a worldwide audience.

You don't have to do what I am doing to expand your presence. You can choose to share your knowledge and teach your skills with those in your immediate circle. It still makes a difference.

♥

**Ponder point**

Life teaches you many things. Sometimes, it simply gives you a perspective on itself. Sometimes, it allows you to acquire specific skills and insights. What has your life taught you that you could share with others?

**Actions to consider**

Speak up the next time you're in a meeting. Your perspective is as valuable as anyone else's.

Share your life story. You never know what someone may learn from listening to your story.

Offer to teach your skills to your co-workers.

Record your observations and thoughts in your journal.

## Forgotten does not mean broken

It's easy to become absorbed in the events of your life. When you're busy, you sometimes forget things or fail to maintain contact with your family and friends.

Your choices may move you away to another city or another country. When that happens, your existing relationships may become dormant as you put them on hold while you work on re-establishing yourself in your new surroundings.

Then, one morning, you wake up and realize you haven't seen or spoken to a particular family member or friend in ages, and you want to reconnect.

When a connection is dormant and not broken, it can be reactivated with a simple telephone call or a visit. Most times, you pick up the relationship from where you left off when you got busy or moved away.

You might feel a need to apologize for neglecting your friend or sister but often you find that no apology is required. They are happy to hear from you and to reconnect.

It's a different story when a connection has been broken. Now there's pain and suffering, misunderstanding, or perhaps guilt, to deal with, depending on how the relationship you want to rekindle was broken.

It takes courage and self-awareness to mend broken connections. You might need to apologize. You might need to forgive. You might need to let go of that imagined slight. You might just need to hug your friend and tell them how much you missed them.

You may need to let the relationship go. Maybe that person has fulfilled their part in your life story or you've fulfilled your part in theirs. If that is what you experience, remember that love is not about possession or attachment.

People come into and move out of your life all the time. Wish them well. Connect with the people that want you in their lives and be open to meeting new friends.

♥

## Ponder point

Do you have any dormant or broken connections with friends and family you want to rekindle?

## Actions to consider

Pick up the telephone and say hello.

Make that visit you have been putting off.

Work out what you need to do to repair a broken relationship that you want to rekindle and then reach out and see whether the other party wants to play again.

Let go of relationships that have reached their expiry date.

Record your observations and thoughts in your journal.

## All events are neutral

It's the stories that the writer of a memoir tells, about the events in their life, that make a memoir more interesting than a mere listing of the events in a person's life.

Your life is no different. It's a series of events that stretches from birth to death.

Many of the events of your life are much like the events of my life. What makes them different is their context and how you and I interpret them as they happen.

When you accept responsibility for your life, you choose to respond to the things that happen from awareness, instead of reacting from fears based on previous experiences or misinformation. This means you see things differently and tell different stories.

Things no longer happen to you. They happen for you to experience or to give you a message to consider.

Events happen. The earthquake, or bushfire, or snow storm, or cancelled flight happens. It's not personal. The personal bit only comes in when you interpret the event. It's your interpretation that generates the story you tell yourself about the event, and it's that story that inspires your response.

It's inconvenient when your flight is cancelled. It's devastating when a natural disaster destroys your house or kills members of your family.

Feeling like that is the human emotional response, but remember that you are not a victim. No-one arranged to cancel the flight just to inconvenience you. No-one arranged for the bushfire just to burn down your house and kill your child.

You can choose to see those events that way and behave accordingly if you wish.

Or you can acknowledge that the event happened and then wonder what lesson it holds for you before you respond. This doesn't mean the event will not be painful but it will give you the opportunity to work through the experience, instead of letting it crush you.

Events may seem to be beyond your control but how you interpret an event and decide to respond is always within your control.

If nothing else helps, remember to breathe or count to ten before responding.

❤

## Ponder point

How do you respond to life's events? Do you wonder why things have happened or do you take it personally?

## Actions to consider

Recall a recent inconvenient event and review your response.

Develop a ritual that allows you a moment to collect your thoughts before responding to events. For example, taking a deep breath and asking yourself a wonder question.

Record your observations and thoughts in your journal.

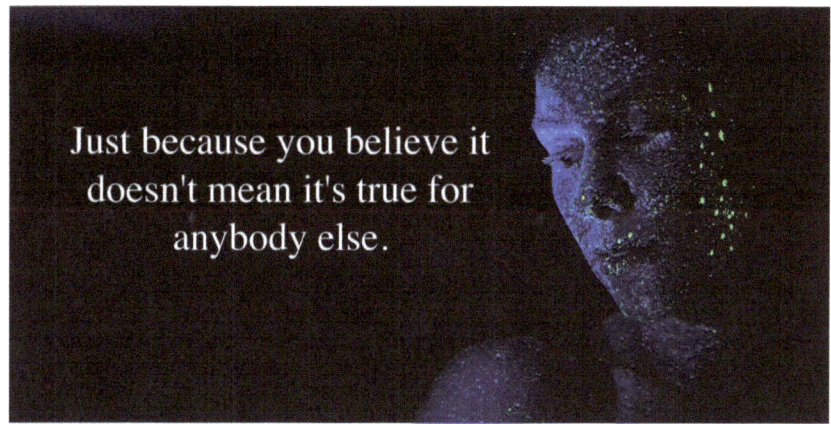

## Just because you believe it

What are our beliefs based on?

Sometimes, we believe what others tell us. We take their beliefs at face value. That happens to us when we're children and we don't have enough information or experience to know any better. Even as adults, we're often faced with a similar situation when some expert is telling us how it is. How many of us, for example, have enough information or relevant experience to know if global warming is man-made or not?

Beliefs are theories based on interpretation of experiences. We share common cultural or scientific beliefs with others but each of us has a personal set of beliefs based on our particular interpretation of our personal experiences.

We have no guarantee that our shared cultural or scientific beliefs are right. What we know is that many of them allow us to operate as societies, as groups of people with common worldviews.

Our personal beliefs are another story altogether. What you believe about yourself may have nothing in common with what I believe about you. Likewise, what you believe about me may not align with what I believe about myself. In fact, what you believe about anyone has more to do with you and your worldview than anything else.

Another way of describing a preconceived opinion or personal belief not rooted in fact is to call it a prejudice.

Our differing beliefs allow us to see things differently. For example, where one person sees a man with a beard, another sees a terrorist, or the person labelled as an illegal immigrant by one commentator is described as a refugee or asylum seeker by another.

An interesting thing about beliefs is that we tend to collect information that supports our beliefs and to reject information that refutes them. In other words, we hear what we want to hear. We see what we want to see. We end up with a worldview determined by our personal beliefs – and fears are nothing more than personal beliefs about negative outcomes.

Our challenge is to become aware of our beliefs and to question them. Are they based in fact or interpretation? And, that is a hard question to answer, given the way our minds work.

❤

### Ponder point

Do you listen to the same radio station, watch the same TV news, or read the same paper every day? Do you ever check alternative sources of information? Do you check facts?

### Actions to consider

Read *Liminal Thinking* by Dave Gray. This is an easy to read book on how we develop beliefs and how we can work with them.

Tune in to some alternative sources of information, for example, try the BBC instead of CNN or read the Washington Post instead of watching Fox News.

Conduct an audit of your personal beliefs and list the evidence supporting each belief.

Record your observations and thoughts in your journal.

## Darkness allows us to see the beauty of our lights

There's a reason we do fireworks at night. The magic of the exploding lights can't compete with the glare of the sun.

When you compare yourself to people more famous or more successful or more whatever than you, your lights are swamped by theirs and you fail to see them.

Step out of the glare. Stop comparing yourself with others, no matter how worthy they may appear to you. Give yourself a chance to see your own value, your own talents, your own achievements, your own lights.

You're not here in competition with anybody else.

When you stop comparing yourself with others, you will see yourself in a new light. No-one else is living your life story. No-one else is doing your life's work. No-one else has your life purpose. You're unique. You are a one off. You don't need to be perfect. In fact, it's your imperfections that make you interesting or give you the edge in pursuing your life purpose or being the lovable person you are.

This can be a difficult habit to break, especially since we've grown up in societies that use comparison to value people. Our parents compare us to our siblings or our cousins. Our teachers compare us to our classmates. Our employers compare us to our co-workers. Our friends compare us to their other friends.

And we do the same. That's how social conditioning works but you don't have to remain a prisoner of your social conditioning.

The advantage of waking up from the dream, which social conditioning only serves to maintain, and accepting responsibility for your life is that you get conscious access to the power of choice, and that allows you to break free from your social conditioning.

So, conduct your self-assessment in the darkness of your own sanctuary, where all the lights that glow are yours.

♥

**Ponder point**

Who have you been comparing yourself with? Why?

**Actions to consider**

Make a list of the things you have achieved in your life. Refer to it whenever you're tempted to think you haven't done anything worthwhile.

Make a list of the things you're good at – your talents. Spend some time honing those talents. It's amazing how good you feel about yourself when you're doing something you're good at.

Record your observations and thoughts in your journal.

## Those who work with love have no need for guns

According to *A Course in Miracles,* fear arises from a lack of love.

People who are afraid believe they need to protect themselves. Some fear strangers in the street, others fear anybody that does not belong to their group, speak their language or believe in their God.

Some people are so consumed by their fears that they are afraid of anybody and everybody.

Interestingly, when you ask people to analyze their fears, it's the stories they tell themselves about other people that they're actually afraid of. For example, a Muslim of any kind is a potential terrorist - until you get to know one as a fellow human. A big black man is a potential thug - until he turns up as the paramedic in an ambulance to attend to your health crisis.

Most of our fears are irrational, especially our fears about other people.

When you consider what actually happens in your daily life, and stop fearing what could happen, most days you discover that you're surrounded by people working with love.

The people around you go about their business with no intention of doing you harm. People are talking to their friends, loving their kids, and doing whatever it takes to put food on the table and keep a roof over their heads.

What intention are you taking into your daily life? Are you like everybody else, going about your business, interacting with your friends, loving your children and earning a living? Are you working with love?

Then you don't need a gun, and chances are you don't walk around with one attached to your body.

Occasionally, someone acts out their fear and kills others in some random, insane act of violence but that does not change the way life works for you – unless you let it.

❤

## Ponder point

Are you afraid of people that do not belong to your group, speak your language, or worship your God?

## Actions to consider

Choose to work with love in your daily life.

Spend some time with someone from one of the groups you fear.

Smile when you meet strangers in the street.

Treat everyone you meet as an equal, despite what they look like or what they're wearing.

Record your observations and thoughts in your journal.

## It's not the truth

Religious beliefs are rooted in ancient, sacred scriptures; books written hundreds or thousands of years ago, which are revered as repositories of truth or the word of God.

Interestingly, no sacred text was written by the Holy One associated with it until the time of Baháʼuʼlláh, who birthed the Baháʼí faith in the late nineteenth century.

The Christian Bible, for example, contains four Gospels; stories about the life of Jesus, telling readers who he was, what he said, what he did, and what happened to him. Each Gospel was written by a different person, not necessarily the person whose name is associated with it, and addressed to a different audience. None of them were penned by Jesus or recorded during his lifetime.

The same is true of most other sacred texts. The Buddha, for example, didn't write anything down either. Everything we know about him and his teachings was recorded by disciples, centuries after his death.

The historical evidence suggests that the stories and teachings in sacred scriptures are based on the transmission of oral teachings, from one generation of disciples to the next, over long periods of time. You need to attribute great powers of memory to both teachers and students to accept the final written product as error free or even remotely similar to what was originally taught.

Then there are the questions that arise from censorship, editing, and the effects of translation from ancient languages into modern words.

There is no denying that sacred scriptures contain universal truths. However, we need to acknowledge that they also contain distortions, cultural norms, and worldviews aligned with their time of origin or translation.

The words in sacred scriptures are not meant to be read literally. Sacred scriptures were not written the way modern books are written. They were written to pass on a belief in the message delivered or revealed by a Holy One.

Often, that message is hidden within a context we moderns no longer understand, and we need to ask for guidance.

♥

### Ponder point

What do you really know about your sacred scripture? Who wrote it? When? Where? Why?

### Actions to consider

The next time you're studying your sacred scripture, take a moment to reflect on the reliability of the words you're reading.

Study the history of your sacred scripture.

Meditate on a scripture passage as opposed to simply reading it, and see if you get a different understanding of what it means.

Record your observations and thoughts in your journal.

## Are you sure it's worth getting upset about?

When someone cuts you off in traffic, do you take a breath and slow down to maintain the safety gap or do you scream abuse and give them the finger?

If you admit to the latter, and let's be honest, we've all done it, isn't it interesting that we let ourselves get upset, irritated and angry at a complete stranger who can't even hear or see us?

Of course, we also get upset with the people we say we love, the people we spend so much of our time with, when they do certain things – even things as simple as squeezing the toothpaste the wrong way.

When we are unaware, and identify with our ego selves, we let so many little things and imagined slights upset us, simply because we take things personally.

We like being right, and we give ourselves permission to be angry when someone does or says something we don't agree with or does something that causes us a slight inconvenience.

Accepting responsibility for your life is acknowledging that you no longer want to live like that. It means you're taking control of your response to any specific situation, by giving yourself a moment to think about it – and it only takes a moment – before you respond.

Remembering to breathe helps. It gives you that little space to ask yourself: are you sure it's worth getting upset about?

Funny thing is, though, most things are not worth getting upset about, and when you stop reacting and start choosing your responses consciously, you feel a lot better.

There are plenty of things we can rightly get upset about. Things like social injustice, corruption, exploitation, discrimination, abuse of power, and war. But simply blowing a fuse and exploding at the TV when you witness them on the news is not the answer either.

If those things upset you, get involved. Become an active warrior for change. Get involved in the political process.

If that's not your calling, remember to breathe, let the moment pass and focus on what you're doing in the moment.

❤

## Ponder point

Are you using mindfulness as a way of being aware of what's going on around you?

## Actions to consider

Make a list of the things you let upset you and ask yourself if anything on that list is actually worth getting upset about.

Practice being mindful as you go about your day.

Allow yourself to pause the next time you encounter a situation that you normally get upset about and see if you can choose to respond differently.

Record your observations and thoughts in your journal.

## Sinking beneath the surface waves of life

If you watch the ocean, all the turmoil is at the surface where the waves are. When you dive into those moving waters, and allow yourself to sink into the depths below those waves, you find yourself in a place of quiet stillness.

Life is much like the ocean. All the drama plays out on the surface layer where you can see and feel what's going on without understanding why any of it is happening.

When you give your attention to the surface layer, life seems chaotic and emotionally draining. There is no peace in the frantic activity most of us think of as our daily life. Most days, there is so much drama you can hardly hear yourself think.

Fortunately, there is a place where you can find peace and quiet, where you can gather your thoughts, and listen to the voice that speaks only love. All you need to do to go there is shift your attention away from the surface and let it sink into the depths within you.

You do that by choosing to stop and take a moment for yourself. You don't have to withdraw from life and go hide in a monastery or ashram. You can do it right where you are, even in the midst of chaos.

This is one role meditation plays in life. Establishing a daily routine of sitting quietly and allowing your attention to go within is the portal into those depths.

For most of us, life is busy. We have things to do, needs to attend to, duties to fulfil, and it's easy to convince yourself that you don't have the time to meditate or sit quietly doing nothing. That's based on a misunderstanding.

Meditation is not doing nothing. It's spending time getting to know yourself. It's spending time accessing the dimensions of life beyond the limitations of the physical. It's connecting to your source and recharging your soul.

Meditation also allows you to review your experiences and see them from difference perspectives. It helps you clarify your thinking.

Of course, it's easier to meditate in a quiet place but you can meditate anywhere, even on the subway or in a busy office. All that's required is a shifting of your attention away from the drama going on around you. Sometimes it only takes a moment. Sometimes, a daily dose of twenty minutes works best.

### Ponder point

We often resist doing something we don't fully understand, or something that sounds foreign. Is meditation one of those things for you?

### Actions to consider

Research various forms of meditation.

Learn to meditate.

Commit or recommit to a daily meditation practice.

Record your observations and thoughts in your journal.

## There are times when you have to wait

'When one door closes, another always opens.'

How often have you heard that phrase when something ended in your life?

My life experience tells me that statement rings true, but sometimes you have to wait for that door to open. Sometimes, you're not ready for that next possibility. Sometimes, you can't see the door until something else shifts, usually your perspective.

These days we seem to always be in a hurry. We have no patience. We want A to follow B, today and not next week. We have fears of missing out, so when one thing, whether it's a job or a relationship, ends, we rush out to start another one. We don't take the time to transition from the ending of what was to the beginning of what could be. We don't allow ourselves any downtime to process what just happened.

That's why the door stays closed.

When you accept responsibility for your life, you take the time required to work out what you want to do next. You take the time to learn the lesson of that ending. You take the time to explore new possibilities.

When fear is driving you, you don't wait for the door to open, you break in and start a new job, a new relationship. But, when you rush things, your immediate fix is usually temporary, and before you know it, you're back to an ending, because Life keeps presenting your lessons until you pay attention, and do the work required to learn from your experiences.

Waiting for that next door to appear and then open requires trust: a trust in the process of life. You need to trust that your higher self, that part of you that remembers it's connected to Source, knows what it's doing.

Sometimes, it's not easy but when you wait, you always find the right door.

## Ponder point

Think of the last time something ended in your life. How did you handle that transition? Did you wait for the door to open or did you break into the first one you came across?

## Actions to consider

Read *Transitions* by William Bridges.

Record your observations and thoughts in your journal.

*Death is an event for observers.
Dying is a life process for participants.*

## Death is an event for observers

Life unfolds as a series of events. The events of your life may be wildly different from the events of any other life, except for death - a common event in every life. There is no escape from the experience of death.

People die every day. When it's the death of a loved one, it can be a traumatic experience. When it's the death of a stranger, it's a news item.

Death's impact depends on your understanding of who you are.

If you identify with your body, then death appears to be the end, and you may suffer from a feeling of deep loss when someone close to you dies, fearing that you will never see them again. You may also fear annihilation at your own death.

If you see yourself as a spiritual being having a human experience, you understand that death is not the end. It's not even something to be feared. It's simply time for the one who has died to hand in their assignment. You know you'll see them again because you understand that spirits are immortal. Only bodies die.

No matter how you see death, it's an experience we will all be having this lifetime. Facing death is one of our greatest fears but it need not be a fear at all.

The fear of dying is based on the stories we tell ourselves about dying; it's not the actual dying that's so scary. In fact, if you've ever been present when someone died, you know it's often a very peaceful experience for everyone involved – including the person doing the dying.

Death is one of those topics not included on the list of things to talk about until it's staring you in the eye or when you're the last member of your cohort still here.

In *The Way of Mastery,* Jeshua tells us that the whole point of his death and resurrection was to remind us that death is not the end. It's just another experience.

Of course, the Church has been spinning stories of hell and damnation to keep us in line – but you don't need to believe any of that. It's just another story.

### Ponder point

Does the thought of your own death frighten you?

### Actions to consider

Read *Many Lives, Many Masters* by Brian Weiss or *Life between Lives* by Dr. Michael Newton.

Participate in a past life regression.

Talk about death and dying as life experiences and not as something to be feared.

Record your observations and thoughts in your journal.

## Look for the beauty – it's always there

Beauty is a gift from Life, an expression of Grace, and it's everywhere – if you have an eye for it. Even a concrete jungle like New York cannot hide beauty as anyone who has walked along the High Line or sat in any of its tiny parks will tell you.

Nature is one expression of beauty most of us recognize. Fortunately, we don't all see a lumber supply yard when we see a forest or a great spot for a marina when we come across a wetland.

Nature isn't the only expression of beauty.

There's an essence of beauty within each and every one of us. Admittedly, it's sometimes hard to see, especially when we project our prejudices upon others, but it's always there.

It's even there within our enemies, within the hearts of all those people we don't understand, and don't want in our backyard.

Not all beauty is out there in the grandeur of the stars or the majestic forests and mountains. Some of it is underfoot, in the mud. Trouble is, we tend to concentrate on the mud, and we miss it.

It's easy to be distracted by what's going on around you; all the drama in the media; the hysteria of your friends; and your own fears about the future. And, in that distraction, you often miss the signs of beauty that are everywhere.

You hear your friend's hurt, but fail to see the warmth in her smile. You hear about what's going wrong in the world, but fail to notice all the things that are going right – even the things going right in your own household.

Give yourself permission to slow down, to look away from everything that is calling for your attention, and look around for the beauty in your life.

It's always there.

❤

### Ponder point

Beauty is in the eye, not of the beholder but of everyone. Look for the light of the divine – it's visible as a sparkle in the eye, the warmth of a smile.

### Actions to consider

Look for the sparkle in each person's eye and the warmth in their smile.

Let your light shine as you go about your day.

Record your observations and thoughts in your journal.

## I am beautiful

Beauty is present within the person who is with you every moment of every day: you. And, that's often the most difficult place for you to recognize it.

You are a beautiful being, despite the stories you have told yourself or heard from others.

We are not talking about the beauty of form, of bodies or faces, which is defined by cultural or advertising norms. That's talking about the packaging without knowing anything about the content.

We are talking about the beauty within: the content which sparkles within all of us, despite our external appearances. This is the light that leaks out and allows others to see our beauty: our true nature, even when we're denying it.

We all have a spark of the divine within us, even when we're committing acts of violence and destruction. Those acts serve to remind us that we are acting out of fear and that we have forgotten who we are at our core.

Sometimes, you have to stop and take the time to learn to love yourself before your beauty becomes visible to you. Sometimes, someone else needs to see it within you before you'll believe it's there.

That doesn't mean that your beauty is not there. It's a pre-installed feature. It's been operational from the moment you were born.

You started life as a beautiful baby, just like everyone else. It's only as you got older and started to believe the stories people told about you that you started to believe you were something that was not beautiful.

Stories are opinions. They are not facts. All storytellers see their world through the filters of their perspectives or prejudices. If they want to see you as something other than beautiful, that's their problem.

When you accept responsibility for your life, you get to be your own storyteller. You get to see yourself and your world any way you choose.

Why not choose beauty?

Why not be beautiful?

## Ponder point

How difficult is it for you to say 'I am beautiful' to yourself?

## Actions to consider

Meditate on the beauty within.

Describe how it feels to know that you are beautiful.

Record your observations and thoughts in your journal.

## Nature is waiting for you

There is something about being surrounded and embraced by nature that restores the soul. You feel a different energy when you're with the trees or listening to the waves breaking on the shoreline.

We have become largely urban and somewhat estranged from nature in our citadels. We spend our days and nights surrounded by man-made structures and man-made sounds.

In some cities, it is never quiet. In fact, there is a frantic energy of activity in our cities, where millions of us crowd together, packed in high rise apartment blocks or side by side in suburbs that sprawl across the landscape, covering up all signs of nature with concrete and planned spaces.

Nature, in all its forms, not only wilderness, offers us the gift of slowing down, the gift of sounds that do not jar our senses or disturb our rest.

It's so relaxing to listen to the repetitive sound of waves breaking or the gurgling of a brook as water flows over and between rocks on its way to a lower level in the landscape.

Thankfully, there will always be somewhere to go to be embraced by nature. It may not be pristine wilderness. It may be agricultural. It may be a regenerating forest or a national park. It may be the park in the middle of the city put there by town planners wise enough to know that we all need nature's gift of restoration.

Maybe it's because I spent my early years in the middle of nowhere, in the quiet open space of inland Australia, that I yearn for nature's embrace after spending time in a city, any city. But, I don't think so.

I'm not the only one looking for restoration away from the hustle and bustle. Even people who have spent their entire lives in cities are tapping into the benefits of spending a few hours or a few days in nature.

It's a gift waiting for you.

♥

**Ponder point**

Some of us resist the call of nature and refuse its gift of restoration, afraid of what we may find there in the quiet.

**Actions to consider**

Go for a daily walk in the park or along the beach.

Give yourself a day or a weekend away from the city.

Record your observations and thoughts in your journal.

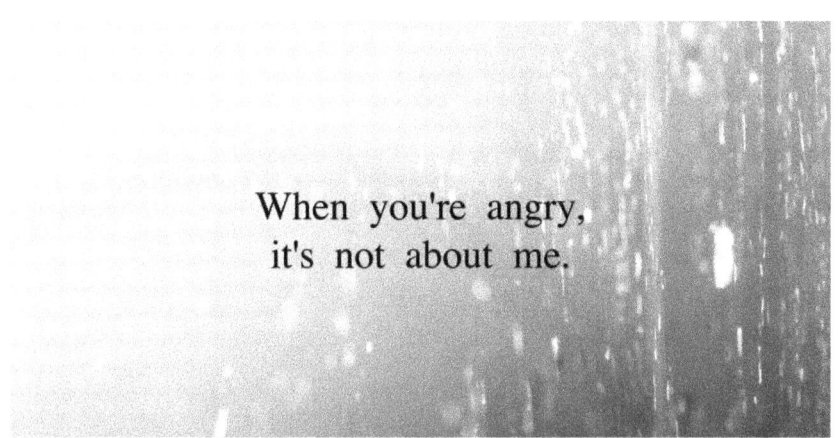

## When you're angry, it's not about me

There is nothing wrong with anger. It's an emotion; a feeling, like sadness or grief or joy. We all experience emotions.

Sometimes, you feel angry when things don't go your way or when people say things that upset you.

Sometimes, you simply have an underlying feeling of being angry with the world or the way things are.

No matter what the apparent cause of your anger, the temptation is to look for someone or something to be angry at. Sometimes, we even use our anger as a weapon in an attempt to get our way or to get preferential treatment.

It's all about interpretation – your interpretation of an event. We've already discussed all events being neutral, so what is it that you have projected onto an event, whether that's something someone said or did or some world catastrophe, that's fired up your anger?

Yes, that's precisely what I'm saying. You're responsible for your anger. If the event was neutral, why are you choosing anger and not something else?

Why are you choosing to take the words or actions personally?

Who knows why they said them, or why they did whatever it was that you let upset you?

In all probability, it had nothing to do with you, so why did you assume it did?

## My Life is My Responsibility.

Even when someone is screaming abuse at you, it's still about them. They've let something get under their skin, and they're using you as a convenient target for venting their anger.

Isn't that what we all do when we're angry?

You don't have to play the game this way.

Accepting responsibility for your life allows you to see that you no longer need to blame others or external events for how you feel. You understand that anger is a chosen response.

Now the question you want the answer to is: why am I choosing this response?

❤

### Ponder point

We all get angry. Sometimes, it seems like there is no other option but there always is.

### Actions to consider

The next time someone pushes your buttons, pause and remind yourself that your response is always about you. Yes, the other person may have done something you feel is upsetting, disrespectful or hurtful – but they are all interpretations, your interpretations.

The next time someone is angry at you, remember that it's not about you before you respond.

Record your observations and thoughts in your journal.

# Appreciate the people in your life – just as they are

We're all tempted to tweak the people in our lives, a little here, a little there, to get them to conform to our idealized version of them. We give them a nudge when their behavior does not meet our expectations, we tell them to think differently when they disagree with us, and to be more careful with their words when we think they have offended someone.

With our children, we do it with the best of intentions – we want them to grow up to be responsible adults. Trouble is, some of us can't seem to stop doing it even when they have grown up.

We fall in love with an amazing person and, almost as soon as the honeymoon is over, we start trying to change them. Some of us don't even wait that long.

It's futile. You can spend years of your life working to change someone you say you love and have nothing to show for it, except their resentment.

Accepting responsibility for your life requires that you acknowledge that there is only one person under your control: you.

Life becomes so much more enjoyable when you accept people just as they are. We all have our foibles. We all have our little annoying mannerisms – even you.

When you appreciate someone just as they are, you actually get to know them for who they are, instead of the person you want them to be.

Yes, he might snore, but he's still a wonderful person. Yes, she might nag you to get things done, but she's still a beautiful person.

Stop wasting your energy on trying to change people. Start enjoying their presence by appreciating them for who they are – warts and all.

♥

## Ponder point

We criticize far too easily. I wonder why we do that? Is it because we are trying to get the world and everybody in it to play by our rules?

## Actions to consider

Listen to yourself when you are talking to your significant other or your children. What are you saying to them? Are you criticizing or appreciating?

Make a list of the things you appreciate about your significant other.

Make a list of the things you appreciate about each of your parents.

Record your observations and thoughts in your journal.

## To be in the present moment

Daydreaming is one of the easiest ways of shifting your awareness away from your present moment reality. At times, it makes sense to think about something else, for example, while you're waiting - but the downside of daydreaming is we often fail to notice what's going on around us.

These days you don't even have to daydream. All you need is a smartphone.

We've all seen people sitting around a table in a coffee shop with their eyes glued to their screens, fingers working away on the next text message or social media post, oblivious to each other. I often wonder why they went to coffee together.

From my perspective, the person sitting next to me, the person sitting across the table from me, is more important to me in that moment than someone I am only connected with through a device.

By not being fully present in moments like those, you're missing most, if not all, of the non-verbal messages that are an essential part of personal communication. You're missing the body language that often tells you more than the words.

Think about the message you send when you only half listen to what your friend is saying because you can't drag your attention away from your smartphone. You're telling her she's not that important to you. You're telling her she's invisible to you. You're telling her that someone who isn't even present in the room is more important to you at that moment.

*My Life is My Responsibility.*

If you reflect on that for a moment, it's easy to see that there is a difference between being distracted and being rude.

It only takes a simple decision to switch off your device when you're with your friends, or when you're out in nature, or when you're anywhere, to allow your mind to be where your body is.

❤

## Ponder point

How much of your present moment reality are you missing out on?

## Actions to consider

Go for a walk and leave your smartphone at home. If that's too big a leap, at least turn it off while you're walking.

Switch your smartphone to silent when you're with friends.

Turn your smartphone off when you go to bed. If you're using it for an alarm clock, switch it to airplane mode.

Record your observations and thoughts in your journal.

# I am not here to judge or be judged

We judge things all the time, so giving up judgment is a challenge.

One form of judgment is evaluation. This is where we consider the pros and cons of a situation before making a decision. We're not talking about giving up that type of judgment. That type is fairly useful in the conduct of daily life.

The form of judgment that gives us trouble is the evaluation of others and of self, where we criticize and often fall into the trap of condemning.

None of us has any idea what is going on within the mind or heart of another person. What that means is that any judgment we make of another is based on our evaluation of their external appearance, and we make that evaluation through the filter of our assumptions about them.

In other words, our judgments are nothing more than opinions based upon our interpretation of reality.

We do the same thing to ourselves. We evaluate ourselves through the filter of our assumptions about ourselves and of reality.

Our assumptions are mostly based on stories and not facts. If we're honest, we will admit that a lot of them are based in ignorance.

It's surprising how similar we all are as human beings when we move beyond the labels we give to each other.

In a similar way, when we move beyond the labels we give to

ourselves, we realize that we are perfect just as we are, and we understand that we do not need to judge or condemn ourselves.

When we accept responsibility for our lives, we remember that we have no need to judge others and no need to judge ourselves.

♥

## Ponder point

When you encounter someone from outside your group, someone who wears different clothes, or holds different beliefs, or speaks a different language, or has a different colored skin, what do you see – a fellow human or a label?

## Actions to consider

Smile and say hello when you meet people in the street, regardless of who they are or appear to be.

Listen to what you say about other people. Would you like to hear people talking about you the way you talk about them?

When you catch yourself being judgmental, just say to yourself: being judgmental. Smile and shake your head, and remind yourself that you've given it up. No need to beat yourself up.

Record your observations and thoughts in your journal.

## Happiness is an inside job

It takes most of us a while to get this one, and we spend a lot of time and energy chasing happiness.

The message of the world is that money, falling in love, reaching your goals, owning a particular house, car, boat or whatever, will bring you happiness. That's a message telling you that your happiness depends on something else. On something outside of you.

Some of us learn the hard way. We accumulate a pile of money, a loving partner, a beautiful house, and lots of things - only to discover that we are still not happy.

Others give up. It all seems too hard and out of reach.

Then, there are those that are happy no matter what they own or what's going on in their lives.

The truth about happiness is that it's not an outcome or a destination. It's a state of being. It's something you choose to be.

You can't have it, bottle it, or sell it. You can't buy it and you don't need to earn it.

Happiness is a gift you give to yourself. It's an attitude you choose to adopt. It doesn't depend on circumstances.

When you decide to be happy, instead of spending your life chasing happiness, you see the circumstances of your life differently. You stop investing so much energy into resisting and complaining, and accept that, for the moment, this is how things are.

My Life is My Responsibility.

This allows you to use your energy to work for the way you want things to be in your life.

Deciding to be happy is deciding not to be defined by your circumstances. It means you can be happy when things are going well for you and when they're not.

We all like being around happy people. Happiness is infectious. It's a gift you can share by simply being happy.

♥

### Ponder point

Happiness is a gift you give to yourself. It's an attitude you choose to adopt. It doesn't depend on circumstances.

### Actions to consider

Read *The Happiness Project* by Gretchen Ruben.

Give yourself permission to be happy.

Record your observations and thoughts in your journal.

## Appreciate what you have

When things aren't going your way, it's easy to overlook the things that have gone your way and fall into complaining.

Appreciating what you have is one way of feeling good about your life.

Take a moment to look around you. Look at the things and people in your life. Notice them. Be thankful for them.

Maybe your iPhone is not the latest version. Be thankful it still works. Maybe your partner is not perfect. Be thankful you have a partner that loves you.

They don't even have to be things you own. They can be things you have access to, things like public gardens, public transport and the local library.

According to the Law of Attraction, you attract into your life the things you give your attention to, so it makes sense to focus on the things you appreciate, as they're the things you see as desirable and want more of in your life.

Sometimes we find ourselves in less than optimal circumstances. An appliance fails at a critical moment, someone lets you down, you lose your job, your partner leaves you, or you get sick.

Accepting responsibility for your life means acknowledging that this is the way things are at the moment and understanding that things never happen to you but for you.

Ask the question: What's the lesson here?

Often, it's only when you understand the lesson that you can appreciate the circumstance that brought it to you.

When you can appreciate both the good and the bad things that happen as you make your way through life, you know you've accepted total responsibility for your life.

❤

### Ponder point

We are surrounded by abundance that we often fail to notice.

### Actions to consider

Take a moment to look around you. Look at the things and people in your life. Notice them. Be thankful for them.

Make a list of the people that you appreciate being in your life.

Make a list of your achievements.

Make a list of all those things you take for granted, all those things you just expect to be there.

Record your observations and thoughts in your journal.

## The secret to forgiveness

We use our interpretations of people's intentions to imagine all sorts of slights and hurts. Your partner, for example, says something that you hear as hurtful. You see attack. You feel violated or taken for granted.

All your partner did was utter a string of words.

That's a neutral event - until you invest it with an interpretation. Instead of asking for clarification, you assume you know what they intended. You end up making a judgment based on a misinterpretation.

When our relationships become strained under the weight of our misinterpretations, we feel a need to forgive in order to restore them.

The temptation is to be magnanimous, to offer the olive branch, to forgive the other for their one or many transgressions.

This is not how forgiveness works.

When you attempt to forgive that way, you end up feeling resentful for swallowing your pride again. You've let them off when what you wanted was an apology. You know you only did it to restore the peace. You still feel that you were right and that, once again, you've been the greater person.

To forgive, acknowledge your misinterpretations and forgive yourself for projecting them onto the other. This involves releasing the other from your judgments and becoming open to seeing them as they are.

*My Life is My Responsibility.*

From the perspective of one who accepts responsibility, feeling hurt or offended is a response.

Instead of holding on to your hurt, wonder why you chose to respond that way in the first place. Finding the underlying reason for your misinterpretation is a first step to being able to respond differently next time.

And, there will be a next time. How else will you know whether you've learnt that particular lesson?

❤

### Ponder point

Instead of holding on to your hurt, wonder why you chose to respond that way in the first place.

### Actions to consider

Acknowledge your misinterpretations and forgive yourself for making them.

Forgive everyone who, in your opinion, has hurt you, by releasing them from the judgments you made about them at the time.

Resolve to ask for clarification instead of making assumptions about the intentions of others.

Record your observations and thoughts in your journal.

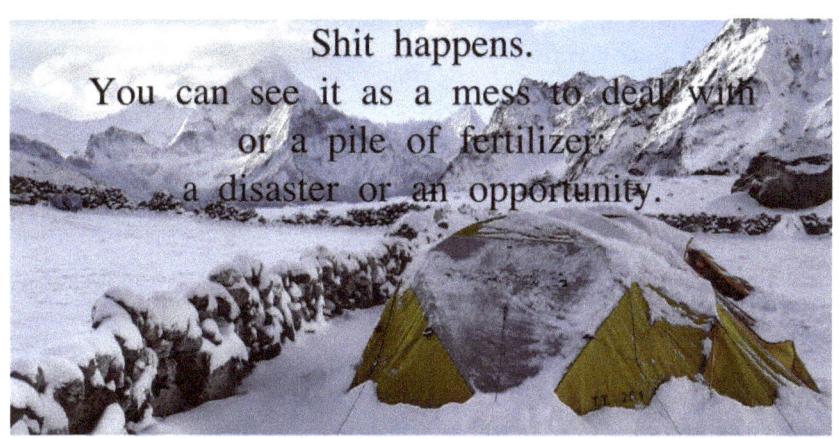

## Shit happens

Wouldn't it be great if, after a moment of enlightenment on the mountain top, everything in your life flowed effortlessly?

From my observations, Life just doesn't play that way. Things we'd rather not encounter still show up, often unexpectedly.

Whatever happens, you are always at liberty to respond any way you choose.

It seems the default human response is to see things in the worst possible light. Maybe this comes from believing life is a struggle against the elements. That may have been true once but, for most of us, it's no longer the case.

What looks like an obstacle is often a solution in disguise, but you will never see that solution if you only concentrate on the obstacle as an obstacle.

If all you see is the pile of shit, you'll never see the fertilizer, simply because your focus is on the problem and not on a possible solution.

All that's required is a slight shift in perception. Instead of asking the usual question: why did this happen to me? Ask a different question: I wonder why this happened?

When you ask that question, you allow yourself the opportunity of seeing a field of possibilities, instead of a disaster or a road block.

Often, all that's required is a willingness to think outside the box or a willingness to put aside your sense of inconvenience.

Sometimes, what appears to be a negative experience is actually an opportunity to solve a problem in the service of others.

In other words, it's not always about you but rather about what you can do for others by applying your unique perspective and talents.

❤

**Ponder point**

What looks like an obstacle is often a solution in disguise, but you will never see that solution if you only concentrate on the obstacle as an obstacle.

**Actions to consider**

Read *The Obstacle is the Way* by Ryan Holiday.

Resolve to wonder why things happen.

Record your observations and thoughts in your journal.

## No-one takes anything from you when they leave

We have so much emotional energy invested in our relationships that we are often devastated when they end.

Death seems to impart such a cruel blow upon those left behind, and when lovers separate, hearts are said to be broken. Some of us sink into deep depression when our significant other leaves the relationship or the planet.

There is nothing wrong with grieving when a relationship ends. That's healthy, and allows you to transition to a new beginning, perhaps with someone else or on your own.

We all survive those endings and, at some point, resume our lives. And, when we resume our lives, we discover that we are in no way diminished. We are still who we always were and perhaps wiser for the experience.

It's a great feeling to be loved by another, just as it is a great feeling to love. But we are not our feelings and neither is our value determined by the attention of another.

It's always a mistake to define your self-worth through your relationships. Your self-worth is determined by who you are, not by who you spend your time with or what you do together.

When people join together in relationships, they bring themselves and that's all they take with them when they leave. They don't take any of you with them, despite what we sing in love songs and write in romance novels. That is all illusion.

When you see yourself as an immortal spiritual being having a human experience, you come to appreciate that no-one ever really leaves. They simply change form or move on to a part of their life story that you didn't sign up for.

We all get to catch up during the semester break between lives, so there is no need to prolong your grief when a relationship ends.

## Ponder point

Are you defining yourself by how you see yourself in relationship to others or by seeing yourself as you are: whole and complete?

## Actions to consider

Read *Many Lives, Many Masters* by Brian Weiss or *Life between Lives* by Dr. Michael Newton.

Record your observations and thoughts in your journal.

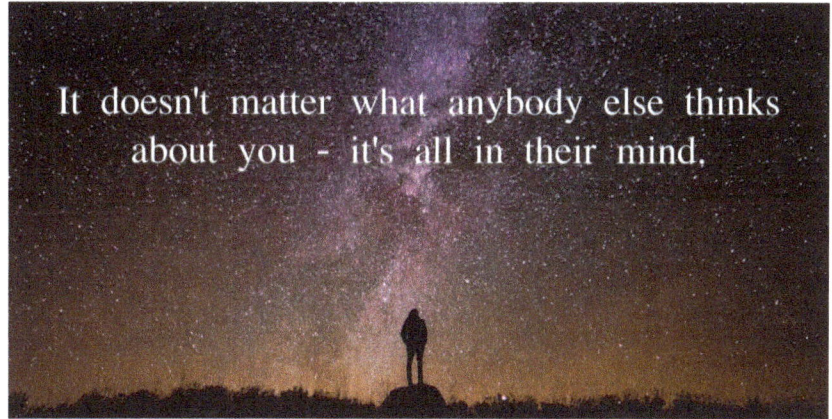

## It doesn't matter what anybody else thinks about you

The only opinion about you that you really need to worry about is your own.

Unfortunately, there is plenty of research out there confirming that we don't think much of ourselves when asked. In fact, there is a whole sector of the economy based around therapies designed to help us get beyond our negative self-talk and images of ourselves.

One of the challenges of starting life as a human is infancy, because you are dependent upon your parents and others, and exposed to their views of who you are and what you're worth. But childhood is not the whole story.

If you survive to become an adult, you get the opportunity to choose your own beliefs. You get the opportunity to decide who you are, despite what your parents and others thought and repeatedly told you.

The challenge is to recognize and seize that opportunity.

Most of us get that opportunity during our mid-thirties, when we have what is known as a mid-life crisis. Some of us have to suffer several rounds before we get it. Others ignore it or try to send it into oblivion with drugs – both legal and otherwise.

A mid-life crisis can be scary but it's also an opportunity to put aside everybody else's opinions about you and to start forming your own.

It's also a time for exploring other philosophies of life, other religions, and other points of view.

If you messed up your first mid-life crisis by refusing to look at things and throwing yourself into your work, it's not too late. Let yourself have another one. In fact, make a conscious decision to explore other possible ways of seeing yourself, the world, and the meaning of life.

My advice is not to settle for what someone else, including me, has told you is the truth about who you are. Their version is all in their mind.

What you want is for the version in your mind to be authentically yours.

❤

## Ponder point

What did you do with your last mid-life crisis? Do you need to give yourself another one?

## Actions to consider

Study *A Course in Miracles*.

Study *The Way of Mastery*.

Read *Waking Up* by Sam Harris

Read *Life on Earth* by Mike Dooley.

Record your observations and thoughts in your journal.

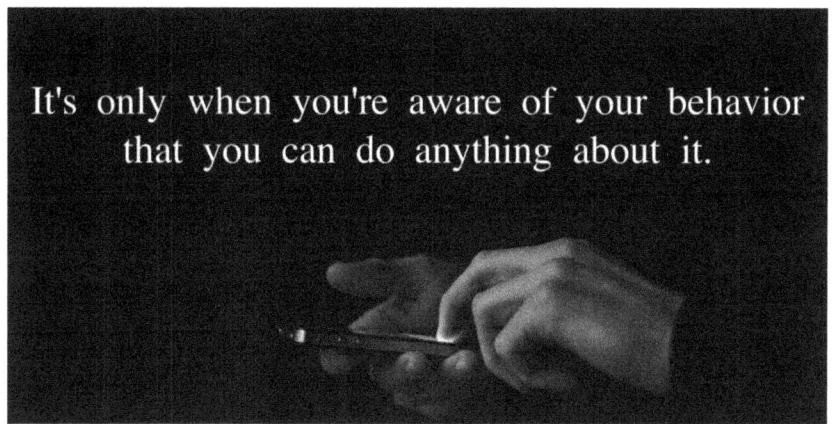

*It's only when you're aware of your behavior that you can do anything about it.*

## It's only when you're aware

Sleepwalkers have no awareness of what they're doing while they're doing it, and no recollection of having done anything while they were asleep. They certainly don't remember the bizarre conversations they had with the person who guided them back to bed.

You can go through life as a sleepwalker, doing things on autopilot without any conscious awareness of what you're doing. Many of your habitual behaviors happen in that zone.

There is another lack of awareness to wake up to beyond habits; the ignorance of the impact of the words you say and the things you do or don't do.

Everything you do sends a signal into your environment. Every time you fail to act reverberates across the silence to everyone watching. Every word you utter tells your audience something about you. Even your choice of words and how you say them is sending a message about your beliefs, attitudes and self-esteem.

Sadly, ignorance does not lead to bliss. It leads to misunderstandings, hurt feelings, confusion, missed opportunities, broken friendships, and angry responses.

Yet, the fallout from ignorance is totally avoidable. All it takes is a little self-awareness, that is, waking up to yourself and your influence on those around you.

Think about the possible impact your actions or words may have on others before you act or speak and take that into consideration when you do.

If you misinterpret the actions or words of others, and, believe me, you do, it's highly likely that others misinterpret whatever you say and do, especially if you don't take them into consideration.

Take the time to become aware of the context of situations you find yourself in, engage with people, and notice how they respond to you.

Not every response will be verbal. Learn to watch for their non-verbal signals. They're often a more reliable indicator of their genuine feelings.

♥

### Ponder point

A sense of self-importance often stops us from being self-aware.

### Actions to consider

Walk a mile in the other person's shoes.

Sit down with a friend or co-worker and ask for feedback on how others perceive you.

Record your observations and thoughts in your journal.

## All endings lead to new beginnings

Sunset is always followed by sunrise, eventually. We only need to endure the night between them to greet the new day.

Life is a series of beginnings leading to endings that lead to new beginnings. We often forget the totality of that sequence and get caught in the trauma of endings.

A relationship ends. We think it's the end of the world, instead of the creation of an opportunity to allow someone new into our lives.

A job ends or a business fails. We think we're ruined or we've failed, instead of seeing the possibility for doing something different.

We have trouble with our endings, despite being able to look back and see that every ending we've experienced led to a new beginning, eventually. Sometimes we had to endure a time of transition first, a dark night of the mind. It's never a dark night of the soul.

Life ends. This is the big one for us.

When someone we love dies, we don't see them starting a new life, so we think it will be the end for us when our turn comes.

For the last couple of thousand years, in the West at least, we've been under the illusion that you only get one life, and then you go to heaven or hell, depending on whether you've played by the rules or not - or that's it, if you don't believe in the rules.

Scientists don't think you'll have a new beginning, except for those folks spending millions on cryonics in the hope they'll somehow be reactivated when Science is able to restart their old body - assuming all those years in storage, frozen in liquid nitrogen, doesn't render them inoperable.

Mystics and past life regression practitioners, on the other hand, tell us we're immortal spirits and that only bodies die. The ending of a life is simply the start of a transition to a new beginning.

### Ponder point

Death is an ending, but it's not the end. It's a transition to a new beginning.

### Actions to consider

Read *Transitions* by William Bridges.

Review your endings and their subsequent new beginnings to identify how you manage transitions.

Record your observations and thoughts in your journal.

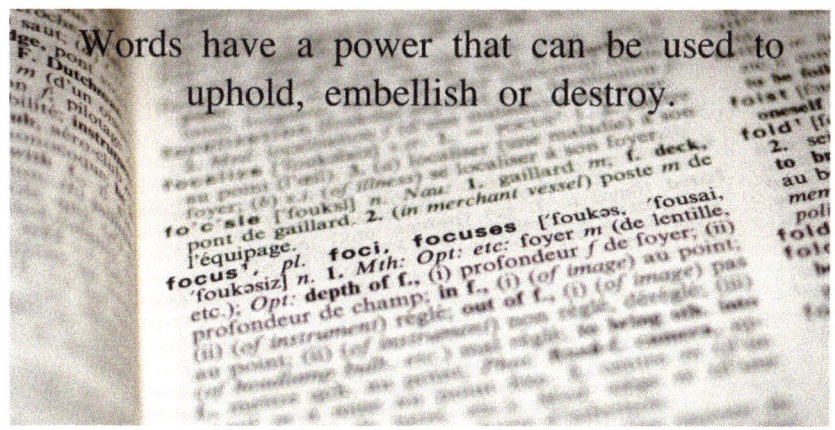

## Words have a power that can be used

Words are how we articulate thoughts and beliefs, how we project ourselves out into the world, and how we describe each other.

Take a moment and listen to the words you use when you talk to yourself about yourself.

Are the words you hear uplifting and reassuring or destructive? Are they words of truth or embellishment?

Listen to the words you use to describe others, especially the words you use to describe those outside your tribe of like-minded associates.

Are you using words as a means of connection or as a weapon of alienation?

The sword is deadlier than the word in hand-to-hand combat but the word is far more effective as a weapon of mass destruction. You only need to listen to a politician or a shock jock practicing the art of fear-mongering, and witness the effect of their words on their audience, to know what I'm talking about.

You need to be aware of the power of words if you are to protect yourself from their misuse – by you and by others. Accepting responsibility means exercising control over your use of words and being awake to the way words can be, and are, used by others.

Be honest about the words you use when you talk to yourself. Commit to telling yourself the truth about how you feel. Commit to using words that are uplifting and reassuring instead of words of doubt and loathing. Tell the simple truth. There is no need to embellish it in an attempt to make yourself look better in the eyes of others.

Think kindly of others and use words that reflect your thoughts. Choose your words carefully and stay aware of the context in which you are speaking.

Be willing to challenge the labels used to denigrate others, especially people who are being portrayed as the enemy.

### Ponder point

How much thought do you give to your choice of words? Do you ever regret how you described someone?

### Actions to consider

Make a list of the words you hear yourself using to describe yourself and write out an uplifting alternative for each negative term you use.

Pay attention to your conversations with others and listen to how you talk about other people.

Record your observations and thoughts in your journal.

## The power of the pause

The button I like the most on my iPhone is the off button. When I use my iPhone as an alarm clock, I switch it to airplane mode before I go to bed. I want to sleep; not be interrupted by incoming email, messages, or someone's urgent need to talk.

I read an article recently about a law being passed in France to allow employees the right to be uncontactable after hours, and how employers were more enthusiastic about it than employees.

Seems we are afraid of being unplugged.

None of us is 'energizer man', no matter how much we might want to be like him. And, we all know what happens to a battery if it's on all the time. It runs out of energy. It goes flat and stops working. It needs to be recharged before it will work again.

The same thing happens to you.

Humans are designed for a daily recharge but that design was signed off way before we started this always on madness. If you're always on, always plugged in, always working, those six to eight hours of sleep terminated by an alarm clock calling you to do it all over again, just aren't enough.

Taking responsibility means looking after your wellbeing. That includes things like diet and exercise, but it also includes getting enough sleep and downtime.

One thing you can do daily to recharge is spend twenty minutes meditating.

Another thing you can do is do what French employees seem to be resisting – disconnect from your work world when you leave the office.

Daily pauses are invigorating but longer pauses away from your devices are vital for your continued sanity.

♥

### Ponder point

When was the last time you spent a weekend away from home? What about a week or more?

### Actions to consider

Read *The Pause Principle* by Kevin Cashman.

Establish a daily meditation practice.

Turn your phone off when you leave work.

Take a vacation.

Record your observations and thoughts in your journal.

## It's okay to start with loving yourself

I remember hearing a speaker on the topic of self-love saying that the problem with Jesus' instruction to 'love your neighbor as you love yourself', is that most of us do.

Everybody in the audience laughed as they recognized the truth in that statement.

We seem to have a few problems with this notion of loving ourselves. I'm not sure how we expect others to love us when we can't love ourselves, but we do.

The popular image of someone who loves himself comes with the negative connotations associated with narcissism and confuses genuine self-love with selfishness.

We are not talking about narcissism or grandiose ideas of self.

When we talk of self-love, we are talking about self-acceptance and treating yourself with loving kindness and compassion.

Loving yourself is essential for developing a healthy self-image and for looking after yourself as you make your way through life. It's what makes it possible to stand on your own feet, to listen to your own counsel, and to reach out to others in love.

When you love yourself, you know it's okay to take time out. You know it's okay to pamper yourself now and then, you know it's okay to take some time to smell the roses and laugh with the kids.

Much of what we do in life is in service of others. All of that comes easily to those who know how to love themselves. They don't feel resentment because they act out of love and not from a sense of duty.

Self-love is a doorway to freedom. It's the portal for getting to know yourself as you truly are.

♥

**Ponder point**

When we talk of self-love, we are talking about self-acceptance and treating yourself with loving kindness and compassion. Are you doing any of that?

**Actions to consider**

Write a love letter to yourself.

Make a list of the things you want to do for yourself and do them.

Record your observations and thoughts in your journal.

> There's nothing wrong with having an opinion - as long as you understand it's just how you see it.

## There's nothing wrong with having an opinion

We all have opinions. Just ask anyone what they think about a topic and you'll get an opinion. Ask ten people the same question and you're likely to get ten different answers.

We're addicted to opinions; mostly our own. We read opinion polls and wonder how anyone could think such things.

When we study a topic or closely follow current events, we think our opinions are well informed. They may be, but they can still be based on misconceptions.

Opinions are like beliefs. They're based on your interpretation of events, and all that information coming into your mind from the outside is being passed through the filters your mind has constructed, which are based on the experiences you've had and the beliefs you've entertained prior to the event.

In other words, you see what you want to see, hear what you want to hear, and dismiss the rest. Psychologists even have a name for this: cognitive bias.

We're all living within mindset bubbles, simply because of the way the brain works. All that information that streams into your central processing unit from your sense organs is run through your mental framework for the world, and then it's presented to your conscious awareness as an interpretation.

The fact that it happens within milliseconds doesn't validate its accuracy.

Everybody forms opinions the same way you do, even experts, but they don't have the same mental framework you have. They may share some common cultural beliefs and experiences with you but their perspectives are unique to them - just as yours are unique to you.

Your opinion is just as valid and just as distorted as anybody else's, so, you need to discuss things if you're ever going to arrive at a consensus view with others.

### Ponder point

Unquestioned acceptance of any opinion, including mine, is fraught with danger.

### Actions to consider

Share your opinions without feeling the need to defend them.

Listen to other people's points of view without feeling you need to agree or disagree with them. They're just alternative views.

Record your observations and thoughts in your journal.

## There are no special roles for spiritual pilgrims

Anyone can walk the spiritual path. It's not restricted to saints or special people. We're all invited.

Spiritual pilgrims perform secular roles while they are on the path. They are not called to withdraw from the world to be spiritual in some secluded place. That's a choice some make, but it's never been a requirement.

Pilgrims recognize that all are equal and that an individual's value is not determined by the role they play in the game of life. Pilgrims know an individual's value is in being the person they are, regardless of the role they play in the game.

The temptation in the game is to be special, to take on a special role, to see yourself as more important because of what you do.

In truth, whether you're playing the role of emperor or slave, underneath the fancy clothes or the rags, you're the same as everybody else. Your experiences might be different but you have the same needs and desires, and the same lessons to learn.

The challenge for pilgrims on the path is being authentic; in being true to themselves as they perform their roles and not letting their roles dictate who they are.

The more power associated with a role the greater the challenge, but don't think that lowly roles are without challenges.

Just as those performing in powerful roles can be corrupted by the illusion of their power, those of us in less glamorous roles can be corrupted by the illusion of being victims of the powerful.

All are called to serve and to accept responsibility for their life. In the repeating circle of life, we get to play the roles that hold the challenges of the lessons we're here to learn.

♥

**Ponder point**

The temptation in the game is to be special, to take on a special role, to see yourself as more important because of what you do. Is this how you see yourself?

**Actions to consider**

Look beyond roles to meet the person standing before you.

Be your best self, regardless of your current role.

Record your observations and thoughts in your journal.

## When you're caught in the drama

There's a military term that's frequently used in the corporate world – taking the helicopter view. It's not hard to work out what it means if you've ever been in a helicopter. It's about being in a position to see the bigger picture. It's why generals usually don't take part in the fighting.

When you're caught up in the heat of the battle, whether that battle is going on in your kitchen with your ten-year-old, on the freeway with other drivers, in the office with your boss, or in your bedroom with your significant other, it's easy to lose sight of the bigger picture when you're focused on the drama of what you're doing.

Our tendency to focus on our problems, to dwell on them, and go over and over them in our minds, often traps us in that drama. It's worse when things are not going our way and we let the emotional pain of our situation blind us to the bigger picture. We lose sight of those who love us. We believe we are alone. We think we have no options.

We are never alone. That's the bigger picture.

There are always options – even when you can't see them.

There is always an alternative view to the one you're fixating on.

There is always someone you can talk to in order to get another perspective.

But, you have to step out of your drama to see those options, and that's not always easy. You have to admit to yourself that you're caught up in the drama of your situation and that you need help.

*My Life is My Responsibility.*

It's always better to take the risk of looking foolish than actually doing something foolish because you failed to look up and see your situation from a different vantage point.

You might not have access to a helicopter but don't let that prevent you from taking a helicopter view of your situation.

❤

## Ponder point

We are never alone. That's the bigger picture.

## Actions to consider

Remember to breathe whenever a situation seems to be too much.

Take a moment to reflect on the totality of the relationship after a difficult moment.

Remember that no matter what the situation looks like now, it will pass. Nothing stays forever.

Record your observations and thoughts in your journal.

## There are no ordinary moments

It's tempting to see life as a series of mundane moments of no consequence, interrupted now and then by a momentous event.

We mark the progression of our years with anniversaries and special days. We count the days down to Christmas or New Year. We forget to live in the moment.

The essence of conscious living is being in the moment, every moment. When we forget to live in the moment, we forget to love in the moment.

Life doesn't do ordinary moments. Life only delivers moments. Classifying them as ordinary is a judgment based on perspective.

Extraordinary things happen when you live in the moment simply because you are present to what's going on around you. You don't miss the silent cues that make up so much of interpersonal communication. You're aware of how your behavior influences others. You notice the subtle fluctuations in the vibration of your energy field when you encounter others or circumstances change.

All it takes to be present in the moment is to give your attention to what you are doing or to the person you are with.

You can fill your moments with the ordinary things of life but that doesn't make those moments ordinary. Greatness arises from present moment attentiveness to ordinary things. Attention to detail produces masterpieces and lasting relationships.

It's often the small gestures, not the great shows of affection to mark the passage of a special day, that make the difference in a relationship.

Every moment is an opportunity to be your loving self.

Every moment is an opportunity to hear the whisperings of your soul as it guides you home.

♥

## Ponder point

Life doesn't do ordinary moments. How any moment turns out is up to you.

## Actions to consider

Make a habit of being present to what you're doing or whoever you are with.

Commit to giving your undivided attention to others when they are talking to you.

Appreciate every moment as a gift and listen for the whisperings of your soul.

Record your observations and thoughts in your journal.

## What is it that you think you can control?

One lesson that it takes many of us a long time to grasp is that there is only one thing we can control – our response to circumstances.

We may very well choose the circumstances into which we are born, with the intention of experiencing our lessons in a particular setting, but once we're in the system, we come to learn that the system runs according to its own rules or laws.

Every time we make a choice, we find ourselves facing unintended consequences, as none of us fully understands the way things work here.

Climate change is our latest collective lesson in unintended consequences. We made a choice, based on our understanding at the time, to burn fossil fuels. Now we know what happens when we do that and can respond accordingly.

We also learn through our individual lessons in unintended consequences.

Initially, we believe that all answers are outside of us, which is why we try to control the circumstances of our lives and the people we live and work with.

We don't actually make any progress until we realize that all the answers lie within.

It's only then that we start to examine our beliefs, and all the thought patterns embedded within our subconscious mind, that have been driving our behaviors.

It's only then that we realize our controlling behaviors have been destroying our relationships, and that our distorted beliefs about reality have been turning heaven into hell.

It's only then that we come to understand that we can change our minds and see things differently.

❤

**Ponder point**

We don't actually make any progress until we realize that all the answers lie within.

**Actions to consider**

Study *A Course in Miracles*.

Commit to a daily meditation practice.

Write out your life story.

Record your observations and thoughts in your journal.

## It's time to take a look behind the curtain

When you look out at the world, you see a picture you have largely created in your mind. You tell yourself that it is reality but, in reality, your mind looks through the curtain of your beliefs.

Unless you pull back that curtain of beliefs, what you see is always a distorted picture. There is truth in the claim that you see what you want to see.

You can't look behind the curtain, to find out what's really there, unless you are prepared to examine and discard your beliefs. There is no other way to get beyond the curtain.

No doubt, you can come up with a list of justifications for your beliefs. You see the world in a particular way because of the experiences you've lived. You even know your worldview has changed with time as you have grown older or had more opportunities to reflect on the meaning of things. I know my worldview has changed – several times.

Every time you question your beliefs, you give yourself an opportunity to see the world through fresh eyes.

Every time you discard a belief, the curtain becomes more transparent and you get to see a clearer picture of reality.

Curtains block the view from both sides. As your curtain becomes more transparent, not only do you begin to see more clearly; you become more visible to others.

Looking behind the curtain is inner work. The curtain is not only a filter - it's also a mask.

*My Life is My Responsibility.*

Taking a look behind the curtain is an invitation to get to know yourself more deeply so you can see clearly and let your light shine.

### Ponder point

Every time you question your beliefs, you give yourself an opportunity to see the world through fresh eyes.

### Actions to consider

Read *The Biology of Belief* by Bruce Lipton.

Read *Liminal Thinking* by Dave Gray.

Give yourself permission to question your beliefs.

Record your observations and thoughts in your journal.

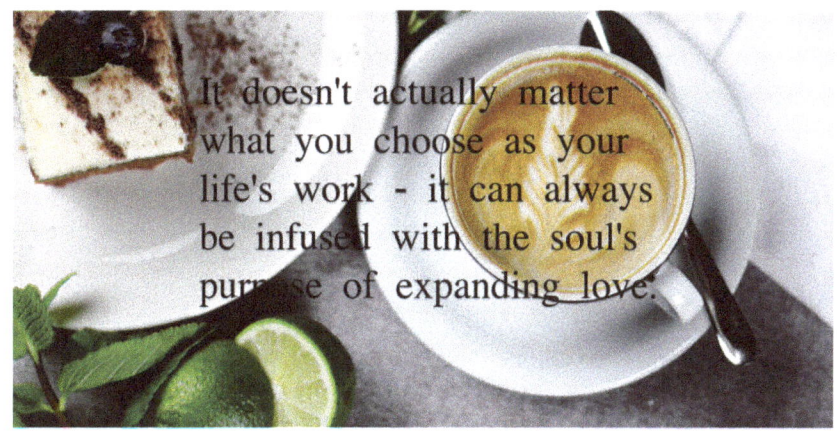

## It doesn't actually matter what you choose

We're all seeking our life purpose. We all want to do something meaningful, to make our unique contribution. There is a whole industry supporting our search for a unique life purpose.

We're all looking for our life purpose in the surface layers of the world of activity, in the world of ten thousand things.

It's important that we do something while we are here. In fact, it's essential in this dimension if we want to keep our bodies alive and in good working order.

The world is set up to allow us to play and to explore different options. It offers us many roles to choose from. There is no particular role that is any more important or of more value than any other, just as there is nothing wrong with choosing a role you enjoy or choosing to move from role to role.

Roles have nothing to do with life purpose. Roles are about experiences. Roles are simply vehicles, means to an end.

You arrived on the planet with nothing but your store of knowledge, and you will leave with nothing but your store of knowledge. It's what you learn while you're here that counts, not what you do to gain that learning.

Your purpose is at a higher level than the mundane activities of the world, and we all have the same purpose: to expand the presence of love.

Stop fretting. Choose something you enjoy doing which suits your talents and interests, and then imbue it with your life purpose.

We are here to learn how to be love in form, and that usually takes on the cloak of service.

❤

### Ponder point

Your purpose is at a higher level than the mundane activities of the world, and we all have the same purpose: to expand the presence of love. How do you feel about knowing that?

### Actions to consider

Look around you. Be the presence of love right where you are.

Whatever you're doing for a living, imbue it with your purpose.

Record your observations and thoughts in your journal.

## You get to choose the level at which you experience life

Until you grasp what accepting responsibility for your life entails, it's difficult to acknowledge that you are choosing how you experience life. It all seems to happen - with no input from you.

Choosing how you experience life does not necessarily mean you get to choose the specific events. It means you are free to choose how you experience the events you encounter. How you respond is always a choice.

There are times, though, when you get to choose the specific event. For example, when you choose a life partner, or decide to accept a job opportunity, or choose to attend a party or a rock concert. Every choice you make in life leads to consequences that become part of your experience. Some outcomes you enjoy; others not so much.

Whenever you decide that you're not enjoying an experience, you have the option of choosing again. You are not obligated to stay and endure unpleasant experiences.

If your choice of life partner doesn't work out, you are free to leave the relationship, despite society's norms and the expectations of others. When a career choice turns sour or you lose your passion for the job, you are free to choose again.

Every choice you make influences your experience of life, even the choice to do nothing, which is often a decision to see yourself as a victim, instead of as someone with the power to choose to respond differently.

Your experience of any life event is determined by how you choose to respond – whether you choose to engage with open mindedness or to suffer through resistance is always your choice.

By choosing conscious living, you're giving yourself the level of awareness required to remember that you can always change your mind, and choose again.

❤

## Ponder point

Whenever you decide that you're not enjoying an experience, you have the option of choosing again. You are not obligated to stay and endure unpleasant experiences. Do you believe this? Are you prepared to act knowing this is always true?

## Actions to consider

Identify an unpleasant situation you're holding on to and consider your options for choosing again.

Remember that choosing again might only mean changing the way you respond.

Choose to be an active participant in your life, not a passive observer.

Record your observations and thoughts in your journal.

## One act of love inspires another

We're all inspired by acts of love. It seems we can't resist love in action, unless we are gripped by fear.

When we act in ways that leave the world a better place, it's always through acts of love. When we act otherwise, it's always because we are acting out of fear.

Every time there is a disaster, natural or man-made, people reach out in love to each other, sometimes across the globe, to offer support and to let those suffering know that they count; that others care about what's happening to them. It doesn't matter what governments do or fail to do when disasters strike, people act.

At some level, we recognize that we are all connected and that we are called to support each other.

When our lives are governed by our fears, we lose our sense of connectedness. We see people from outside our community as others – not us. It's in these moments that those living consciously are called to inspire others through acts of love.

Sometimes, it's not easy.

At times, it takes great courage to show others love in action but that action is always worth it and, often, it's that action of love that melts hearts, dissolves fears, and inspires people to reach out and help strangers in need.

Our purpose is to expand the presence of love.

My Life is My Responsibility.

You can't do that if you refuse to act out of love.

## Ponder point

When we act in ways that leave the world a better place, it's always through acts of love. When we act otherwise, it's always because we are acting out of fear. Are you choosing love or fear?

## Actions to consider

Smile at strangers in the street.

Offer a helping hand instead of walking by.

Support organizations like Medecins Sans Frontieres.

Record your observations and thoughts in your journal.

## One person living authentically allows others

You spend the first part of your life constructing a persona to present to the world. You select a role and then act it out, keeping your true self hidden.

If you're like the rest of us, you probably tried out a few personas before deciding on the one you'd hide behind. Perhaps you have multiple personas and select the appropriate one depending on who you're with and what you're doing.

We start being selective with our personas when we're young. I remember my mother talking about her street angels and home devils. We act differently with the people at work than with the people at home. We show a different face to our lovers than to our enemies.

When you stop seeking approval from others and start living authentically, you give yourself permission to stop hiding behind your masks. When you live authentically, you are the same person no matter where you are or who you're with.

When you live authentically, you let your light shine no matter where you are or who you're with. You're more relaxed, and you don't let the behavior of others upset you, as you once did.

People notice, and that allows them to become more relaxed around you, especially when they realize you're not judging them and they don't need to put on their airs and graces to impress you.

They come out from behind their masks and you get to see them as they really are, in all their beauty.

Living authentically means being vulnerable; you have nothing to hide and nothing to hide behind.

Something quite wonderful happens when we interact authentically with each other. Life flows; and we go with the flow.

❤

**Ponder point**

When you live authentically, you let your light shine no matter where you are or who you're with.

**Actions to consider**

Read *Falling Upwards* by Richard Rohr.

Read *Daring Greatly* by Brene Brown.

Review the way you behave when you're with different people.

Commit to being yourself.

Record your observations and thoughts in your journal.

*Sometimes you get to plant seeds that germinate long after you're gone.*

# Sometimes you get to plant seeds

It doesn't matter what field you choose, it takes time for new ideas to catch on. It's not uncommon for new ideas to be regarded as heresy when they are first proposed, only to become the generally accepted truth in a later age. Think about the idea of the earth orbiting the sun. Galileo suffered for planting that seed. We take it for granted as being the truth.

You've probably noticed that this book is a packet of seeds. Maybe some of them sounded like heresy when you first read them. A few of them did to me, when I first encountered them, but I gave them time to germinate, so I could decide which ones were flowers and which ones were weeds.

I remember Richard Rohr once saying something like, it's amazing how what you think is a weed changes the longer you look at the garden of your mind.

The fate of the seeds on these pages depends on the quality of soil into which they fall – your state of mind. If an idea encounters an open mind, it's likely to take root and prosper or at least be given a chance to germinate before being identified as a weed. If that same idea encounters a closed mind, it will suffer the fate of a seed falling on rocky ground. It won't get a chance to germinate, let alone grow into something wonderful.

I know I'm planting seeds, just as those who walked this path before me planted the seeds that have germinated into this book of insights.

Now, you have an opportunity to do the same, and to be patient while the seeds you sow take root in the minds of those you share them with.

Modern day mystics are called to share their insights. Not to impose them nor to insist on doctrines or that their way is the only way. We share to encourage others to question the beliefs they have taken on from the culture, religion, and society in which they live. We share to awaken.

We're a little like Jesus or the Buddha in that respect.

### Ponder point

We share to awaken. How open are you to sharing your inner beliefs with others? Are you prepared to risk planting seeds, even when others might laugh?

### Actions to consider

Share your insights without expecting any particular outcome.

When you come across a new idea, give it time to germinate instead of dismissing it out of hand.

Record your observations and thoughts in your journal.

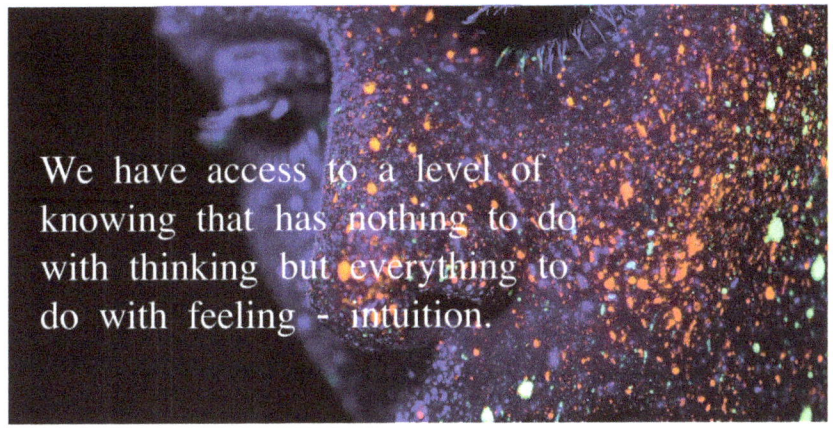

## We have access to a level of knowing

Mandatory schooling, ushered in by the Enlightenment, focuses on what we refer to as left brain thinking. The logical and the analytical, all that fact-based stuff. If your schooling was anything like mine, you were probably taught that if you couldn't see it, touch it, or measure it, it didn't exist.

The only time that was glossed over in my education was during physics and chemistry when we were discussing atoms and chemical reactions. We couldn't see the atoms but we were taught that the atomic model was the only way scientists could explain how things happened, especially things that happened in test tubes.

Then we got into quantum physics. I still don't understand how that works, and I'm not sure anyone else does either.

What I've discovered in the years since, though, is that there is another way of knowing, a way that doesn't rely on observations of the external world, a way that doesn't even rely on logic or analysis. Sometimes, you simply know stuff without doing any research.

You have a problem. You ask for help and wait for an answer. Some might call that prayer. Others would call it talking to yourself. We all do it, regardless of what you call it.

The answer might not come straight away, but it always comes, often when you least expect it or when you're focused on doing something else. We have a name for the source of those answers – intuition.

Ever walked into a room and just known something was wrong, or met a person who smiled and greeted you pleasantly enough but you got a feeling that said watch out, this guy is not genuine? That's your intuition in action.

I've learnt not to dismiss those feelings, and I encourage you to pay attention to yours.

❤

## Ponder point

We have access to a level of knowing that has nothing to do with thinking but everything to do with feeling – intuition. Do you have the courage to access that level of knowing?

## Actions to consider

Read *The Intuitive Way* by Penney Peirce.

Take note of those thoughts that pop into your mind when you're in the shower, and act on them.

Sit quietly, and intentionally ask for guidance on a particular issue, and write down the first thought that comes into your mind.

Record your observations and thoughts in your journal.

## There is a much bigger plan at play

Every one of us has a limited vision of reality.

Some of us restrict our vision to that of one lifetime – you're born, you have fun, and you die. End of story.

Others want to extend that story with graduating into eternal bliss in heaven or falling into eternal damnation in hell. If you're a Catholic, you also have the option of spending a period of post life suffering in purgatory, before final graduation into heaven.

Then, there are those who see a totally different picture, of being an eternal soul on a never-ending journey of growth and development. This is the picture of many lifetimes, many bodies, and many places.

I don't think you can get the whole story from here but if you stop focusing solely on the surface layer of life and tap into the divine, you'll start to get a feeling that there's a lot more to it than you'll ever be able to imagine.

That's not easy for those of us educated in the West. We have to let go of some of our cherished ideas. We have to let go of any notion of being in control. We have to trust the divine.

One of the lessons Jeshua teaches in *The Way of Mastery*, reminds us that we got to where we are by following our plan, which is nothing more than a dream, and that we have to wake up to who we really are before we'll ever get a glimpse of what's really going on in what we call Life.

We spend so much time and energy attempting to control the

circumstances of our lives. We dream up so many plans, set so many goals, and we do most of that without taking the time to go within and remember the reason we chose to be born, this time.

**Ponder point**

Every one of us has a limited vision of reality. Why would you choose to accept a vision written down by someone two thousand years ago?

**Actions to consider**

Explore some alternative viewpoints on the meaning of life.

Imagine what it might mean for you if you are an eternal soul having a series of incarnations.

Review the events of your life and join the dots, and consider if you've been guided or left to your own plans.

Record your observations and thoughts in your journal.

## Life is a field of possibilities

When you discuss your upcoming life with your spirit guides before incarnating, you consider a range of possibilities. Each possibility offers a different set of lessons. In the end, you choose a life with an initial set of circumstances as your starting point, with the intention of completing an assignment designed to enhance your development.

When you're born as a human, no matter how many times you've been here before, you start again, and spend years getting some measure of control over the body-mind you incarnated into, and developing a personality for operating in this dimension.

Then, you're faced with that field of possibilities again. What are you going to do with your life, now that you have the hang of it, gotten an education, and figured out you need money to pay for the things that keep the body alive?

In some cultures, those choices are made for you. In others, you have to make them for yourself.

In times gone by, your choices were restricted by the station your family occupied in society and the occupation of your father.

As education of the masses has swept across the globe, more and more of us are faced with making our own choices. And, it's not only career choices.

You have the power of choice when responding to any life event, and there are often many ways you can respond. The danger is thinking you have to respond to an event the same way every time it occurs.

*My Life is My Responsibility.*

If you're not vigilant, your responses become habitual and you lose sight of the field of possibilities, which is always spread out before you.

Conscious living is taking the time to always look up and consider the possibilities before acting.

❤

## Ponder point

You have the power of choice when responding to any life event, and there are often many ways you can respond. Are you ready to choose again?

## Actions to consider

Do something different.

Speak to someone you usually ignore.

Ask if there is another way you could do something.

Review your career choice.

Read outside your usual range of interests.

Record your observations and thoughts in your journal.

## The spiritual journey happens in the here and now

It's tempting to believe the spiritual journey is solely an interior experience; something you engage in within the solitude of your sacred space.

In times past, mystics retreated to monasteries and ashrams, far away from the noise of the world and ventured into the unknown, seeking union with the divine.

Today's mystics, people like you and me, are called to a different spiritual journey. We are called to remember that we are one with the divine, but we are also asked to walk openly among the throngs of humanity where we can be seen.

We are in the streets, the offices, and the factories of the world, right there where everybody else is. We are called to fully engage in being human, in being incarnate, right where life is happening.

Spirituality is not about seeking some ecstatic experience on the mountain top. It's about being fully present to your experience of life. It's about being fully attentive to those you are with. It's about letting your light shine for others to see, instead of hiding inside, where it's safe.

Today's mystics are wayshowers, called to awaken others and remind them that they are more than they think they are.

We can't do that if we stay safely within a monastery or keep our insights to ourselves. We are called to walk with others and to live our

*My Life is My Responsibility.*

insights in the here and now of everyday life.

## Ponder point

We are called to engage fully in being human, in being incarnate, right where life is happening. Where else can you be you?

## Actions to consider

Start a book club to discuss this and similar books.

Share your insights with your friends.

Integrate your spiritual insights into your daily living.

Commit to living consciously.

Record your observations and thoughts in your journal.

# Further reading

*A Course in Miracles* by Foundation for Inner Peace

*Daring Greatly* by Brene Brown

*Falling Upwards* by Richard Rohr

*Life between Lives* by Dr Michael Newton

*Life on Earth* by Mike Dooley

*Liminal Thinking* by Dave Gray

*Many Lives, Many Masters* by Brian Weiss

*The Biology of Belief* by Bruce Lipton

*The Happiness Project* by Gretchen Ruben

*The Intuitive Way* by Penney Pierce

*The Obstacle is the Way* by Ryan Holiday

*The Pause Principle* by Kevin Cashman

*The Way of Mastery* by Shanti Christo Foundation

*Transitions* by William Bridges

*Waking Up* by Sam Harris

# A note from Peter

*My Life is My Responsibility: Insights for Conscious Living* is my third book of insights. I hope you enjoy working with the insights and receive a few of your own.

I see sharing these insights, which have come to me over years of meditation and study, as part of my life's work. You can help create a greater awareness of them by writing a review and telling your friends about the book.

You can find details about my other books and read my blog on www.petermulraney.com, where you can subscribe to my monthl newsletter 'Insights from a crime writing mystic' and download a free copy of *A Question of Perspective*.

If you're interested in my crime writing, you can also join my Crime Readers Group and download a free copy of my novella: *Deadly Sands*.

Finally, thank you for buying the book.

Peter Mulraney

# Photographic credits

Chapter 1: Alex Krivec

Chapter 2: Hartmut Tobias

Chapter 3: Peter Mulraney

Chapter 4: Lee Scott

Chapter 5: Peter Mulraney

Chapter 6: David Marcu

Chapter 7: David Marcu

Chapter 8: Peter Mulraney

Chapter 9: Alessandro Viaro

Chapter 10: Peter Mulraney

Chapter 11: Frances Gunn

Chapter 12 and cover image: H Heyerlein

Chapter 13: Thaddaeus Lim

Chapter 14: Karl Fredrickson

Chapter 15: Ben White

Chapter 16: Jay Ruzesky

Chapter 17: Austin Schmid

Chapter 18: Jayme McColgan

Chapter 19: Peter Mulraney

Chapter 20: Peter Mulraney

Chapter 21: Sebastian Boguszewicz

Chapter 22: Peter Mulraney

Chapter 23: Death to Stock

Chapter 24: Andreas Ronningen

Chapter 25: Kamesh Vedula

Chapter 26: Anton Darius

Chapter 27: Paul Talbot

Chapter 28: Tongle Dakum
Chapter 29: Christopher Windus
Chapter 30: Wolfgang Lutz
Chapter 31: Jan Schulz
Chapter 32: Greg Rakozy
Chapter 33: Gilles Lambert
Chapter 34: Yoal Desurmont
Chapter 35: Romain Vignes
Chapter 36: Aaron Burden
Chapter 37: Steven Spassov
Chapter 38: Bench Accounting
Chapter 39: Himanshu Singh Gurjar
Chapter 40: Evan Kirby
Chapter 41: Simon Hattinga Verschure
Chapter 42: Iren Petrova
Chapter 43: Maxime Amoudruz
Chapter 44: Toa Heftiba
Chapter 45: Seth Doyle
Chapter 46: Annie Spratt
Chapter 47: Abi Lewis
Chapter 48: Adrian Moran
Chapter 49: H Heyerlein
Chapter 50: Greg Rakozy
Chapter 51: Nigel Lo
Chapter 52: Yns Plt

# Other Titles by Peter Mulraney

**Writings of the Mystic**

Sharing the Journey: Reflections of a Reluctant Mystic.

A Question of Perspective

I Am Affirmations: The Power of Words.

Beyond the Words: Reflections on I Am Affirmations

Mystical Journey: A Handbook for Modern Mystics

**Inspector West series**

Deadly Sands: An Inspector West Short Story

After

The Holiday

Holy Death

Whistleblower

Twisted Justice

The East Park Syndicate

Inspector West Collection One

Inspector West Collection Two

**Stella Bruno Investigates**

The Identity Thief

A Gun of Many Parts

Bones in the Forest

A Deadly Game of Hangman

Taken

Fallout

The Identity Thief Collection

The Fallout Collection

**Living Alone series**

After She's Gone

Cooking 4 One

Sanity Savers

Living Alone (Collection)

Living Alone Journal

**Everyday Business Skills**

Everyday Project Management

Everyday Productivity

Everyday Money Management

**Novella**

The New Girlfriend

**Sharing the Journey Coloring Books**

Mandalas

Mandalas by 3

**Sharing the Journey Coloring Journals**

Sharing the Journey Coloring Journal

Sharing the Journey Coloring Journal ~ Discovery

Sharing the Journey Coloring Journal ~ Reflection

www.ingramcontent.com/pod-product-compliance
Lightning Source LLC
Chambersburg PA
CBHW061203010526
44110CB00064B/2670